A Walk in the Garden

GO BEYOND ME
BOOK ONE

SUSAN STIVER

A WALK IN THE GARDEN

Go Beyond Me Series, Book One

Copyright © 2024 by Susan Stiver

All rights reserved.

Scripture taken from *THE MESSAGE*. Copyright © 1993, 1994, 1995, 1996, 2000, 2001, 2002. Used by permission of NavPress Publishing Group.

Scripture quotations taken from the (NASB®) New American Standard Bible®, Copyright © 1960, 1971, 1977, 1995, 2020 by The Lockman Foundation. Used by permission. All rights reserved. lockman.org

All photos taken by Susan Stiver or used with permission.

Cover Design by John Bryll Pulido website: brilliantcover.com

Interior Design and Publishing by RLS Creativity Publishing https://web.actionera.com/RLSCreativity/

Paperback ISBN: 978-1-998542-04-8

E-book ISBN: 978-1-998542-05-5

Dedication

This book is dedicated to my husband, Don,

who, through his love, has encouraged me

to be who God created me to be.

Acknowledgments

Thank You, Father God,
for all that you have poured into my life
through family and friends,
for joy in the midst of it all,
and for the overflow through which
You will continue to bless others.
May Your Name be lifted high,
forever and ever. Amen.

Butchart Gardens

Contents

Lake Lure Flowering Bridge

Invitation

_Enter the Garden with your eyes wide open to see the
beauty of life as it unfolds in poetry and
ponderings of one who has been in awe of her
Creator since her earliest memories._

_Some of the writings are whimsical, some are heart
cries, some are queries, and some are just plain
down-to-earth everyday stuff that makes
human existence real._

_Come step into the wonder of this writer's world,
and enjoy the walk in the garden._

Lake Lure Flowering Bridge

Go Beyond Me

What I see I can't paint.
    What I hear I can't write.
Ideas are all jumbled,
    And the colors aren't right.

Please take what I see
    And translate it to art.
Help me paint with my hand
    What I feel in my heart.

Then take the pen
    Far beyond what I think
To express from Your Heart
    On paper with ink.

Please go beyond me –
    Beyond boundaries and fear,
So I can paint what I see
    And write what I hear.

Thank You, Papa God!

Butchart Gardens

Butchart Gardens

Stretched
Beyond endurance
SNAP!

Open
No boundaries
Limitless

Biltmore Gardens

Life is...

A journey that is as individual as fingerprints, DNA, snowflakes –

no two are alike.

Life is...

A creative masterpiece with a design all its own –

the blueprint drawn by The Master Craftsman.

Life is...

Highs and lows, ebbs and flow, dark and light, day and night.

The single point?

Life is!

F L T 💣

*Has anyone ever asked you about your **F L T**?* 💣
　　Or better yet, tried it out to see
What triggers the thing in each situation,
　　Or identifies the variable in each equation?

*You see, **F L T** 💣 is a fact of life –*
　　Mostly evident in periods of strife.
It surfaces when we least expect it
　　And have no time to circumvent it.

All too soon it's in our face –
　　Trying to disqualify us in the race.
It pushes, shoves and shoves some more,
　　Then it's an all-out tug of war.

It does it's best to make us fall;
　　To trip and stumble, or hit the wall.
It pressures us beyond our strength –
　　It's ever testing our fuse's length.

*Your **F L T** 💣 may be just like mine,*
　　Or it could be one of a kind.
Once you've defined it, good news – there's a fix,
　　But only when, you add God in the mix.

By waiting on God our strength is renewed
　　And all our enemies have been subdued.
In His love, He pulls us out of the rut –
　　And by His hand the fuse is cut!

In the Spring

Things are young in the spring of the year
    And as I watch I can see God here.
They bloom and grow with a beauty rare.
    In all this wonder I can see God's care.
Through the summer they spend their life
    Without a toil, without a strife.
Then colors change in the fall of the year –
    A work of art – I know God's near.
Coldness falls as a blanket of frost,
    While summer warmth is now but lost.
Lifeless they lay through the winter snow,
    Yet they do not die – this fact I know!
For in the spring new life begins,
    And I can watch God's work again.

Daniel Stowe Botanical Gardens

Structural Systems

In all the earth there is an order,
And a structure to all things.
In life it's more than buildings,
It's a peace that knowledge brings.

It's wisdom to those who seek it;
Understanding to those who call.
It's hope in the face of danger,
And strength to scale the walls.

It's far more than a building –
It's a foundation sure and true.
It's God's Structural System,
And His perfect plan for you.

"'For I know the plans that I have for you,' declares the Lord, 'plans for prosperity and not for disaster, to give you a future and a hope. Then you will call upon Me and come and pray to Me, and I will listen to you. And you will seek Me and find Me when you search for Me with all your heart.'"

Jeremiah 29:11-13 (NASB)

Heart to Heart

Sometimes we can't communicate
 As often as we should.
Were it in my power
 I would change that, if I could.

I'd spend every minute, every day
 Trying to express
What would be so clearly said
 With a gentle sweet caress.

I'd tell you of my love for you
 And the fullness of my heart.
I'd pledge to you my faithfulness
 And strive to do my part.

I'd let you know a thousand ways
 What your love means to me.
The eagles I'd see far below
 As I'd soar above the trees!

A gift more precious than silver,
 A treasure greater than gold –
How blessed am I, my beloved,
 For I have you to hold.

So when we're apart and out of reach,
 Please know I'm there with you,
And trust that our hearts communicate
 When spoken words are few.

From the Clay

In His goodness and wisdom
    God works with His hands.
He sculptures a life –
    A most wonderful plan!

A vessel of worth
    Far more precious than gold,
If it's left in His hand
    To shape and to mold.

The Potter has need
    Of the pots that He makes –
To serve the lost world
    For His Kingdom's sake.

But the pot so inclined
    To stay on the shelf
Is of no use at all
    Outside of itself.

So break it He must
    To start over again
To re-sculpture that life –
    A most wonderful plan!

Praise be to the Potter,
    His love does abound
As He molds and shapes us
    From the clay of the ground.

Picking up the Pieces

It hurts! I can feel it.
    This pain has got to go!
My heart's in a million pieces—
    More than you could know.

My eyes are blurred with crying
    That never seems to end.
This wounding feels much deeper –
    Inflicted by a "friend".

My thoughts take off to wondering
    What if this or that?
Was any of this really real?
    Or was it all an act?

Emotions flood my being.
    Confusion steps in too.
How could I have been so blind?
    How could I have trusted you?

Somewhere along the way
    I lost sight of what is right.
Then I lost my footing
    And stumbled in the night.

Then in all His goodness
    Abba Father said "That's enough."
He held my hand and whispered
    "It's gonna be hard, but you're tough!"

Yes, my Dad is picking up all the pieces.
    He'll make me better than new.
I'll come out stronger for the pain
    And a whole lot wiser too.

*But you know what else? I **can** feel!*
    And in spite of all the pain –
I'll choose to praise my loving God
    And I'll dance with joy in the rain!

"God made my life complete

    when I placed all the pieces before him.

When I got my act together,

    he gave me a fresh start.

Now I'm alert to God's ways;

    I don't take God for granted.

Every day I review the ways he works;

    I try not to miss a trick.

I feel put back together,

    and I'm watching my step.

God rewrote the text of my life

    when I opened the book of my heart to his eyes."

Psalm 18:20-24 (The Message)

"God pick up the pieces. Put me back together again.

You are my praise!"

Jeremiah 17:14 (The Message)

The Great Transformation

Father, Thank You that

Into darkness –
  You speak light.
Into death –
  You speak life.

Out of sorrow –
  You bring joy.
Out of joblessness –
  You employ.

Out of sickness –
  You bring health.
Out of poverty –
  You bring wealth.

Out of weakness –
  You show strength.
Out of short sightedness –
  You show length.

Out of hopeless –
  Into hope renewed!
Out of ourselves –
  And into You!

Thank You for so great a transformation!
In Jesus' name, Amen!

Can You Hear My Pain?

Can you hear my pain?
My heart and soul are crying out!
Can you hear it? Listen!
With every breath my being shouts!

The pain's so great it robs me
Of my voice and all my words.
The silence is so deafening,
But still you haven't heard!

Helpless in my sorrow
And hopeless for a sign,
In my desperation
I choose to cross the line.

Have you heard me yet?
I'm fading, my vision growing dim.
A face, a voice, confusion;
Little recall of where I've been.

So dark the night before me,
But I'm here now. Someone heard.
There's life ahead because my God
Heard my unspoken words.

"Let your gentle spirit be known to all men. The Lord is near. Be anxious for nothing, but in everything by prayer and supplication with thanksgiving let your requests be made known to God."
Philippians 4:5-6 (NASB)

Silence Speaks

In the silence of my little room
*   I shed a tear, and think of home.*
My heart gives way to emptiness
*   As here I sit in quietness.*

Then, Silence spoke in muffled tone
*   With a loneliness all its own.*
It seemed to say, "Why must you cry?
*   Tis only time that passes by.*
It will, you know, it doesn't wait.
*   It hurries by and makes you late.*
You have no reason for that tear.
*   No good excuse to give for fear.*
Look at the grief that I must bear –
*   I have no home, no one to care.*
Instead, I board with Emptiness
*   And share with him my loneliness.*

Now, look at you – you have such things.
*   You know the love and joy Life brings.*
The smile upon your parents' face –
*   I envy you – you have a place!*
Don't be so blind! Wake up you fool!
*   Don't be as stubborn as a mule!*
Instead, be thankful you can be
*   A friend with lots of company."*

Remember

"Remember" – You say, "Remember!"
    Those things I would like to forget;
Those times of hurt and failure,
    All those deeds I most regret.
Yet still You say, "Remember!"
    Lest I should stumble and fall again.
"Remember" the path on which I strayed,
    Or that door I entered in.
A door to someplace secret
    On a path to doom and death.
How could I ever lose sight of
    The very One who gives me breath?

Lord, free me from the darkness
    And the cold that fills this room.
Bring me to Your brightness,
    And birth me from the womb.
Bring forth a child so humble
    That I would spend my days
Remembering Your lovingkindness
    And lifting Your name in praise.
Then grow me past the hurt and pain;
    Your hand has brought me through.
Use those things for other's good,
    Bringing glory and honor to You.
Yes, You say, "Remember!"
    And may I never forget
That You my God are Lord of all,
    And in love, You paid my debt.

Pearson Falls

"'For I know the plans that I have for you,' declares the Lord, 'plans for prosperity and not for disaster, to give you a future and a hope. Then you will call upon Me and come and pray to Me, and I will listen to you. And you will seek Me and find Me when you search for Me with all your heart.'"

Jeremiah 29:11-13 (NASB)

My Father's Lap

When I feel discouraged
Into Your lap I crawl.
I bring to You my heavy heart
Along with tears and all.

I'm welcome there. I know it,
Because You told me so.
Your love for me so apparent –
Where else would I go?

In Your face I see mercy.
You accept me as I am.
You hear my heart cry deep within,
Then You share with me Your plan.

A plan for hope and a future,
The promise of strength and peace,
The wisdom to discern evil,
Rejoicing that does not cease.

Then from Your lap I leap again
Ready to face the task,
Knowing that You'll be with me,
If I just seek and ask.

Freedom

Freedom to come and go as I please
Freedom so quickly lost
Freedom to choose the path for me
Freedom at any cost

Freedom to lose for selfishness
Freedom so hard to reclaim
Freedom that cost my Savior's life
Freedom with so much pain

True freedom is mine if I want it
Freedom all mine for the taking
Freedom just taken for granted
Freedom bestowed for the breaking

Freedom in bars and a single cell
Freedom without an appeal
Freedom to abide in my Savior's love
Freedom at last to be real.

"So if the Son makes you free, you will be free indeed."

John 8:36 (NASB)

Prison Ministry 2004

Our Choice

Why are pages ever left blank?
    Because we fail to fill them with words!
Why are battles left unfought?
    Because we fail to draw our swords!

Why are prayers unanswered?
    Because we fail to ask and look!
Why are lessons still unlearned?
    Because we fail to open The Book!

Why are lives so scattered and lost?
    Because we fail to grasp what's dear!
Why are questions always endless?
    Because we fail to stop and hear!

A thousand times in a day
    We're given the right to choose.
We choose between what's right and wrong;
    We choose to win or lose.

Why are dreams un-realized?
    Because we fail to do our part!
Why are choices short of best?
    Because we fail to see God's heart!

Serving Vessels

You made a difference by stepping out
 And stepping up to the plate.
You moved right out of your comfort zones
 And not a moment too late.

You saw the work that lay ahead
 And you put your hand to the plow.
The tables were set, the guests were served.
 God moved in the here-and-now.

For us, it was a Banquet
 And an Auction to prepare.
For God, it is an expression and
 A vision to be shared.

So through these earthen vessels –
 So worthless on their own,
God poured out His blessings
 And made His mission known.

Now it's up to all who heard
 To process all these things.
For us, we'll keep being vessels
 In the hands of our Master and King!

Thank you, Asheville Team!
Champions for Life
Kick-Off Banquet July 9th 2005

"Immediately Jesus made His disciples get into the boat and go ahead of Him to the other side to Bethsaida, while He Himself was sending the crowd away."

Mark 6:45 (NASB)

"Get in the Boat!"
Mark 6:45

Can you hear Him beckon?
> "Come, get in the boat!"
Urgently He calls us –
> No time for a vote!

To embark on this journey
> We have to get in,
Quick, push off the shore.
> It's time to begin.

To get there from here
> We have to leave land.
Set the boat afloat and
> Take the Master's hand.

Leave all that's familiar,
> Seek the Father's heart.
He provides the boat,
> But we must do our part.

Rain Down

Blessed beyond measure
    How can I explain?
We called for God's fire
    Then watched as it rained –
His mercy, His power,
    His forgiveness and grace.
He poured out His Spirit
    And filled up this place.

Forget the umbrella
    And don't run for cover.
Let His glory rain down
    As we lift up each other.

Then wet to the bone
    And so glad that it rained,
Let's embrace the future -
    Our lives ever changed.

"But I have trusted in Your lovingkindness;
My heart shall rejoice in Your salvation.
I will sing to the Lord,
Because He has dealt bountifully with me."
Psalm 13:5-6 (NASB)

Weathering the Storm

Did I ask for the storm?
    No, but it came.
Did I ask for the thunder?
    The lightening? The rain?

Did I ask for my world
    To be turned upside down?
Did I ask for my heart
    To be stomped on the ground?

Did I ask for the hurt?
    The deceit and the lies?
Did I ask for the hate?
    The disdain? The despise?

Did I ask for betrayal?
    Denial or loss?
Can I fathom the pain
    Christ felt on the cross?

He experienced all this
    And so much more.
Nothing compares
    To the burden He bore.

Did I ask for the storm?
    No, but it came.
I will choose to give thanks
    In my Savior's Name.

Butchart Gardens

<u>The Hiding Place</u>

Beyond my control,
    But not out of Your hand,
Chaos and confusion –
    Not part of Your plan.

Traffic and delays –
    All part of the test.
Anxiety and fear –
    Overcome by Your rest.

In the hustle and bustle
    I can hide in Your calm.
Tired and weary –
    Your peace is the balm.

Restored by Your mercy,
    Refreshed by Your grace,
So grateful You've brought me
    To Your hiding place.

Higher

How can I know what "Higher" is
*   If I've never experienced low?*
How can I know the depth of God's love
*   If I'm not willing to go?....*

Go to the place of the hurt and the pain;
*   Go to the place of the storm and the rain;*
Go to the place of the blemish and stain;
*   Go to the place to be made whole again.*

It's there at Your feet, I see Your face;
*   There on the ground, I know this place.*
Face down in the dirt – I receive Your grace.
*   With my whole being, it's You I embrace!*

For out of Your love, You birthed me again.
*   You call me Your daughter, Beloved, and*
*   friend.*
You took what was broken, to fix and to mend –
*   Take me higher still to world without end.*

Father, Thank You for the journey.

A Higher Calling

Calling me higher –
    Do I have to go up?
Calling me higher –
    It seems so abrupt.
Calling me higher –
    Is there no other way?
Calling me higher –
    From night into day.

Calling me higher –
    My fear escalates.
Calling me higher –
    No time for debate.
Calling me higher –
    Beginning to climb.
Calling me higher –
    The choice must be mine.

Calling me higher –
  Ascending the stairs.
Calling me higher –
  To a place of prayer.
Calling me higher –
  So grateful You called.

Calling me higher –
  To stand on the wall.
Calling me higher –
  My love ever new.
Calling me higher –
  My life only You.

Breakthrough

Father, this is out of my league,
 Far beyond the bounds;
So unworthy to approach
 Even the fringe of Your Holy Ground.

Father, what am I seeing?
 What are these words that I hear?
What is the heaviness in my heart?
 Why am I brought to tears?

A flood of emotions
 Burst from without and within.
Speechless in Your presence –
 You cause my soul to cry out again.

Break through the walls
 That inhibit Your praise.
Answer the prayers
 That Your people raise.

Between heaven and earth
 You meet me in this place.
Let Your glory rain down.
 Please, let me see Your face.

Abba Father, I praise You
For now I see
The depth of grace and love
You have for me.

Jesus, You are the sign,
You are the wonder!
You've broken through this cloud
That I've been under.

You've unlocked a door
And it's not by chance –
The tears are now joy,
And You are my dance!

Bridal Paradigm

Awaken Your bride –
    Sound the alarm!
Quicken her heart;
    Save her from harm!

Replenish the oil;
    Call down the flame!
Set her afire –
    Forever changed!

Burn all consuming –
    Yet unconsumed.
Make her the offering -
    A fragrant perfume.

Set her desire
    On You alone.
Hear as the Spirit
    And the Bride say, "Come".

Make us a ready bride, and come quickly LORD!

"The Spirit and the bride say, 'Come.' And let the one who hears say, 'Come.'"

Revelation 22:17 (NASB)

From

From the depths of the Wilderness,
       You bring the song.
From the dry barren places –
       The rain all day long.

From the broken vessel,
       You pour new wine.
From Your abundance,
       From now for all time.

From our emptiness,
       Your vast wealth.
From our disease and sickness,
       Your wholeness and health.

From the beginning
       To time without end.
You are our Savior,
       Redeemer and Friend.

SOAKING

Seeking God

Offering praise

Acknowledging who He is

Kneeling before Him

Intent to hear His voice

No other gods – God alone

Giving thanks

"Then they cried out to the LORD in their trouble;
He saved them out of their distresses.
He sent His word and healed them,
and delivered them from their destructions.
Let them give thanks to the LORD for His lovingkindness,
and for His wonders to the sons of men!
Let them also offer sacrifices of thanksgiving,
and tell of His works with joyful singing."
Psalm 107:19-22 (NASB)

The Heart Cry of the Healing Room Team

Pressing through
    To give You praise!
Breaking the chains –
    Our hands we raise!
Moving past
    Familiar turf –
Bringing Your Kingdom
    Down to earth.

One voice.
    One accord.
One heart –
    All for the Lord.
Driven to seek You.
    Pressing through.
The Pearl of great price –
    Nothing but You!
Anointed to serve.
    Gifted to heal.
Giving You glory!
    Blood bought and sealed!

Heart Memories

It's not up to me to save your memories
    It's hard enough to save my own.
The things I wanted most to catch –
    The Fuji camera's blown.

The beauty and the wonder
    Are left behind me now.
I wrestle with my foggy head
    Trying to remember it all somehow.

The majesty of the mountains
    And the colors of the sky.
The faces of the people –
    O Lord, I want to cry.

Don't let me forget a single thing
    You showed me in that place.
From the beauty in each flower
    To the stories on each face.

Like the wonder of a little child
Reading eyes and pinching skin –
Let me be so bold as they –
To reach out from deep within.

You've shown me it's so much more than whole –
It's every little part.
What I saw – a camera could not hold –
So You imprinted them in my heart.

Thank You Father God
for the work You have done in Mission fields.

God's Creative Work

Get in the boat.
  Row to the deep.
Watch for the storm –
  Waves that are steep.

Hold to the oars –
  Row as if one.
Head t'ward the Voice
  That beckons us come.

Follow His lead –
  Move with His heart.
Walk on the water –
  Watch the waves part!

Dance in the deep!
  Joy in the waves!
Celebrate life –
  With the Ancient of Days!!!

Splash in the foam;
  Ride in the curl.
Be tossed and turned –
  God's creating a pearl!

Called Up and Called Out

Called to the mountain
  The Summit, The Top.
Called to climb higher –
  Don't quit and don't stop!

Called to be different
  And called as His own,
Called out of the crowds –
  But never alone!

Called to discern between
  The wrong and the right.
Called out of the darkness,
  And into His light.

Called into service
    And called into rest –
Called by the Master –
    Called to be blessed.

Called – can you hear Him?
    Called as His sheep;
Called as His children –
    Our souls He keeps.

Called to give answers
    When put to the test.
Called to give praise –
    He gives us His best!......

Called and so grateful!
    Called out of the mess.
Called to just love Him –
    How could we do less?

Called to move mountains –
    Believe and not doubt!
No higher calling –
    Called up and called out!!!!!

God, Get Our Attention

Whisper on the wind.
    Speak with the waves.
Thunder from mountains.
    Echo in caves.

Flicker like candles.
    Blaze like the sun.
Send rays through the clouds –
    Cause darkness to run.

Twist through tornados.
    Pour like the rain.
Tickle with feathers.
    Make the earth quake.

Break all the rules
    Of rhythm and rhyme.
Break through our senses.
    Cross over the lines.

Take us beyond
    What we see and can hear.
Awaken our being
    To know that You're near!

Down But Not Out

Sitting and Sitting
  To ease the pain.
Moving so slow,
  Avoid hurt again.

Too much to push,
  Too impatient to wait.
Like a horse in a race
  Pinned in the gate.

Head strong to finish,
  But too weak to move.
Attempting the impossible
  With nothing to prove.

Trying to listen
  Just wanting to hear.
Thoughts are all jumbled
  Like a forest to be cleared.

Systems mis-wired,
  Kinks here and there.
At a time most inconvenient –
  No fun and no fair!

In the chaos and pain,
  Forced to stop, look, and see.
Papa stops what He's doing
  To take care of me.

Wedding Blessing

May God be your Strong Tower
  Your blessing, your light.
May He be your provision;
  Your joy in the night.
May He be the swift answer
  When the hard questions come.
May He be wide-open arms
  Into which you will run.
May He be your true counsel;
  The map for the way.
May He be the fulfillment
  For all that you pray.

Blessing your wedding
  is only the start.
Blessing your marriage
  Is the delight of His heart.

Rewired

The circuits are twisted –
    All tangled with kinks.
Some are all criss-crossed –
    It's so hard to think.

Wires are disconnected –
    The splices are split;
Some are barely touching,
    And they're arcing a bit.

A miss-fire here
    And an over charge there –
No rhyme and no reason,
    No fun and no fair!

A head that's all foggy,
    A heart running a race –
Both in need of rewiring
    And resetting the pace!

Let's call into order
    This jumbled up mess.
Let's lean into GOD –
    And let Him do the rest!

Master Electrician –
    He sure knows His trade.
Rewired to praise Him –
    So wonderfully made.

Go the Distance

How far do you go
    To make the connection?
How much do you give
    To express your affection?

How will you know
    when enough is enough?
How will you measure
    When it's too little? Too much?

Is the question, "how?"
    Is it "what, who, why, when?"
Is it dollars and cents?
    When's the best time to begin?

The answers are simple –
    To the ends of the earth;
Everything you've got,
    And for all that you're worth!

The who, what, why, when
    Will answer the how.
Go the distance with love.
    No better time than now!

<u>*Molly*</u>

How do you say, "Goodbye" to a friend,
    Who God has placed in your heart?
How do you look her straight in the eye
    Without the tears that start?

How do you convey the love that you feel
    For the person God created her to be?
How do you say, "Wherever you go
    You'll always be kin to me."?

How do you leave without looking back?
    Maybe I will, or I won't.
How do you say, "Goodbye" to a friend?
    The answer is easy – You don't!

<u>*The Eye of the Storm*</u>

The storm rages wildly –
     The rain and the wind.
The tornado whirls madly –
     When will it end?
Caught in the turmoil,
     Debris all around;
Tossed in the whirlwind –
     Thrown to the ground.
Crawling to safety,
     I move to the eye.
The storm moves around me,
     But I'm safe inside.

The Father then whispers,
     "Come close to My heart.
Release all the pieces,
     And I'll do My part.
Your heart cry I've heard.
     Your burdens I'll lift.
Let go of the struggles.
     Lay hold of the gift.
The gift is the peace
     In the midst of the storm.
The gift is each day
     From the day you were born.
So stand in the eye
     Of the storm and you'll see
Just how much you are loved,
     And treasured by Me!"

Let Me Fly

Don't lay me out,
    Or lay me under.
Turn me loose
    And let me fly.

Sing a song
    And dance with joy.
Oh, but please
    Don't cry.

I knew this day
    Would finally come.
I'm leaving
    Earthly things.

What a joy to see
    My Savior's face,
And thank Him
    For my wings.

Tapestry of Love

God knows the end from the beginning –
Even every breath we take.
He watches as we move through life –
Even the wrong turns we make.

He patiently waits while He watches.
He whispers hope in our ears.
The path straightens out as we listen,
But the journey often takes years.

Then as we look back we realize
Everything was supposed to be.
By His design, He used every part
To complete His Love Tapestry.

"I want you woven into a tapestry of love, in touch with everything there is to know of God. Then you will have minds confident and at rest, focused on Christ, God's great mystery. All the richest treasures of wisdom and knowledge are embedded in that mystery and nowhere else. And we have been shown the mystery!"

Colossians 2:2-3 (The Message)

Pull Together

Pull together -
    Not apart!
Don't let this time
    Unravel you.
Look deep within
    Your wounded heart,
And do
    What you must do.
Seek God
    To find the answers.
For surely
    He will come.
He promised
    He will be there,
If to Him
    You run.
Guard your heart.
    Watch your step,
Lest you trip
    And fall.
For in Him
    We're surely kept
If on Him
    We call.

What if...?

What if I could touch the sky?
　　What if pigs 🐷 could really fly?
What if night would never come?
　　What if roadrunners couldn't run?

What if trees 🌲 grew upside down 🙃?
　　What if shade could not be found?
What if rivers ceased to flow?
　　What if fireflies didn't glow?

What if I were you 😜 and you were me 🤪?
　　Oh how silly that would be!
But you are you and I am I –
　　And we both know that pigs can't fly.

What if this poem would never end?
　　"What-ifs" are endless, my dear friend.
So with all that, I say good-bye 👋.
　　P.S. I CAN really touch the sky!

"I can do all things through Christ who strengthens me."

Philippians 4:13 (NASB)

Upside Down

Upside down and inside out -
    Is this what life is all about?
Blurred vision and distorted sound,
    Dizzy on this Merry-Go-Round!

Cold is hot, and hot is cold.
    Old is young, and young is old.
Bones are brittle, hair is white.
    Night is day, and day is night.

Backwards! Just backwards in every way –
    Even the thoughts and words we say.
The seasons change – spring, summer to fall
    Winter comes and goes – that's all.

Half the Page

Half the page –
      What's up with that?
Where did it go –
      The other half?

To the store
      As a shopping list?
Or to the trash
      With an extra twist?

Silly thing
      To make you wonder;
Half the puzzle
      On which to ponder.

My Only Need

The shop owner bid me "welcome"
　　As he turned on the "OPEN" sign.
He opened the door and motioned
　　For me to come inside.

The shop was filled with treasure –
　　Stocked from ceiling to floor.
He bid me to come in farther
　　And through another door.

The building seemed to be endless –
　　A most peculiar place.
The isles went on forever –
　　Transcending time and space!

All I'd ever need was there –
　　Except a place to hide!
*He made it clear, "that was a **want**"*
　　*"Your only **need** is to ABIDE!"*

Seasons Change

Seasons change
And so must I –
With last-stitch effort
I have to try

To see what lies
Around the bend
So I don't repeat
Mistakes again.

Through ups and downs,
The snags and falls –
I must build a house
And bring down walls.

Open the doors
And windows, too.
Clean out the rubble –
So much to do!

Busy, busy –
Too busy I say.
Life wasn't meant
To be lived this way.

There has to be
A time to be still –
Time for my soul
To be refilled.

Without that time
The inner me dies.
Be gone the beguile
Of the enemy's lies.

Be gone, I say,
You haven't a chance,
For the inner me
Has chosen to dance!

In the quiet I hear
The sound of His voice,
The beat of His heart
For me, His dear choice.

A love so amazing,
How can I resist?
It's time to rethink
My priority list.

Yes, seasons change
And so must I.
I choose to live
before I die!

Butchart Gardens

Let the Child Win

Is it recess yet?
    Let the child win.
Quiet the adult –
    Be a kid again.

Time out from the chores;
    Lay down the load.
Go climb a tree,
    Or pick up a toad.

Hike in the woods;
    Play in the leaves;
Splash in the creek,
    And grass-stain your knees.

Run till you're breathless;
    Laugh till you cry;
Skip down the sidewalk;
    Ask all the "why?s"

Then lay down to sleep
    With sweet, sweet rest
Knowing the child won,
    And you've done your best!

Out of Sync

Out of sync –
        What am I here for?
You've given me space –
        Did I miss the door?

I should be up –
        The sky's the limit!
But instead
        I'm flat on the floor.

Deal with me –
        Fix what's broken.
Awaken my soul
        Before it's no more!

Better yet –
        Just do me in.
Pick up the chips
        And tally the score.

"No score." You say?
        "This isn't a game...
Its life,
        And there so much more!"

"Pick yourself up,
        And dust yourself off.
Go find what I
        Created you for!"

Another Chapter

Are books ever really finished?
    Not while there's still pen and ink.
Not while the author still has a breath,
    And the passion to write as he thinks!

What about art for the artist?
    Is there a limit to color and space?
Not while there's canvas and brushes,
    And a world full of life to embrace!

Butchart Gardens

All the More

Constant battle, constant fight.
     Defeating wrong, defending right.
Facing liars with the Truth,
     Warding off the evil brute!

Praying for the width and length
     Of all Your might and all Your strength,
Drained I fall down at Your feet,
     The enemy is Yours to defeat.

So take away my anxious thoughts;
     The victory's won, the battle fought.

Let me see the day ahead
     Without a worry or a dread.
Show me what You have in store,
     And I will praise You all the more!

"And we know that God causes all things to work together for good to those who love God, to those who are called according to His purpose."

Romans 8:28 (NASB)

All Worthwhile

When love was young
        And so was I,
I'd lay and watch
        The clouds go by.

No thought of pain
        Or stormy days –
Only "ever-afters"
        And "always".

But life – it happens
        And time flies by,
Just like the clouds
        Up in the sky.

Until one day
        I finally see
The whole of life
        In front of me.

The hurt, the pain
        Were all worthwhile –
Replaced by joy –
        The frown – a smile!

Lake Lure Flowering Bridge

Treasure in the Waiting

Treasure in the waiting –
What should I see?
Is there something to hear?
Or should I just "be"?

It's time to be quiet –
Set my soul to rest.
Don't settle for "better" –
Choose only the "best".

Stay still, but move forward.
"Not possible," you say.
In Kingdom dynamics
There's no other way!

So I sit, and I wait;
I breathe, and I pray.
I move when God tells me
In full battle array.

Thank You, Father, for times of waiting in preparation for the battle.

Worship Haikus

Peace and grace beyond
all we ask or imagine
God's love anointing

Up from the mire
Freed from the chains of the past
Washed clean as the snow

Undone by your love
Expand my heart to receive
More mercy and grace

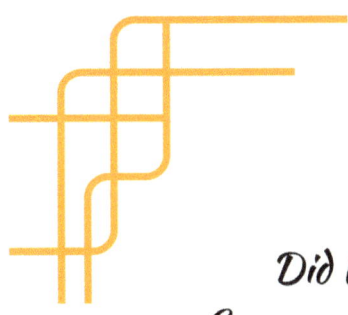

Did I hear your voice?
Come and steal my heart away
Let me see your face

❧

Healing resonates
Each beat of the broken heart
This resounding joy

❧

My brother will praise
He will dance with abandon
And fall to his knees

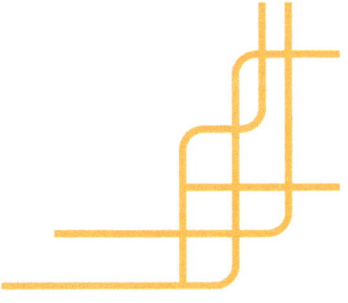

Biltmore Gardens

One More Door

One more door I've yet to find.
    One more mountain left to climb.
One more song still left to write.
    One more battle left to fight.

One more day to seek Your face.
    One more time in Your embrace.
One more whisper in my ear.
    One more touch to know You're near.

In all of life, there's always more –
    More of what You have in store.
More for me to celebrate;
    More on which to concentrate.

More to know the depth of You.
    More to see the height of You.
More to feel the love of You.
    More to worship all of You.

Now I know that "one-more-door"
    Is my heart You're longing for.
So with abandon all the more
    I yield to You my one more door.

<u>*With a Wing and a Prayer*</u>

How can I go higher
    When I have no wings?
I sit and I wonder,
    I ponder these things.

Like a bird takes to flight
    I so want to soar.
I look to the sky,
    But I'm still on the floor.

I don't want a plane,
    Or mechanical tools,
Instruments to read,
    Or classes in school!

I just want to fly
    With my wings in the air.
My heart takes a leap
    With a wing and a prayer!

Break Into My World

Why do I hesitate?
What do I fear?
Is it what I can't see?
Or that I can't hear?

Is there a wall between
My head and my heart?
What stands in the way
Of pursuing my art?

My arms are not broken
But lay at my side.
The brushes too heavy -
I just want to hide.

Break into my world;
Break through in my soul!
Break me out of this prison
Before I grow old!

My Precious Stones

Be transparent before Me.
I will make of you precious stones –
Gems of My Glory.
I will be color that invades
And explodes through you.
Don't muddy the water
Or cloud the sky.
Be still and know that I AM
And I will break forth.
In your stillness
I will move.
I will transform.
I will create.
Behold My Glory.

Love,
The Master Craftsman

Masterpiece

Bask in the moment -
    This season in time.
Take in the sights,
    The sounds, and the signs.

Bask in the beauty –
    The mountains and trees.
Feel the sun on your face,
    And the soft gentle breeze.

Bask in the color –
    It's intensity and hue,
The warm and the cool
    Of the reds and the blues.

Bask in the knowing
    From the depths of your heart –
You're part of this masterpiece,
    A fine work of art!

Ghost Ranch NM 2019

<u>*Ireland Whispers*</u>

From seashore and beaches
    To mountains we climbed,
Each of us thinking up
    Limericks and rhymes.

Joy filled the coach
    Of our grand silver steed.
Through the sun, rain, and fog
    We moved in God's speed.

Over the greens and
    The landscape of stone,
The ground whispered gently,
    "Welcome back home."

Under Shepherds

Call forth the shepherd
    For the bleating sheep.
One who'll gather the lost,
    And a vigil watch keep.

Bring forth the shepherd –
    The sheep to lead,
From out of the wilderness
    Into pastures to feed.

Send forth the shepherd
    With the courage to fight –
Protecting the sheep,
    Defending the right!

Cover the shepherd
    With all that is true –
Wisdom and strength
    As he follows You!

Thank you, Good Shepherd, for the under shepherds.

Tend the Temple

Creator, God,
    You built this frame,
Then by Your word
    Your Spirit came.
You filled this house
    And none could stand.
"Tend the Temple!"
    Was Your command.
I heed Your word,
    And bend the knee,
I pray with all
    humility:

Thank You, Lord
    For mercy and grace.
Thank You, Lord
    You hear from this place.
Thank You, Lord
    With praise I come.
All glory to You,
    Most Holy One!

"You realize, don't you, that you are the temple of God, and God himself is present in you? No one will get by with vandalizing God's temple, you can be sure of that. God's temple is sacred—and you, remember, are the temple."

I Corinthians 3:16-17 (The Message)

Sow and So

Sow? Sow what?
   Seeds for the future, hope for tomorrow,
   Joy for today!
So? So what?
   So the world will know the love of God
   For all mankind!

"So will My word be which goes forth from My mouth; it will not return to Me empty, without accomplishing what I desire, and without succeeding in the matter for which I sent it."
Isaiah 55:11 (NASB)

Butchart Gardens

Dedicated to the brave bunch of seniors who met regularly to encourage, and exercise with, each other. Thank you for the joy and laughter we shared trying to stay healthy.

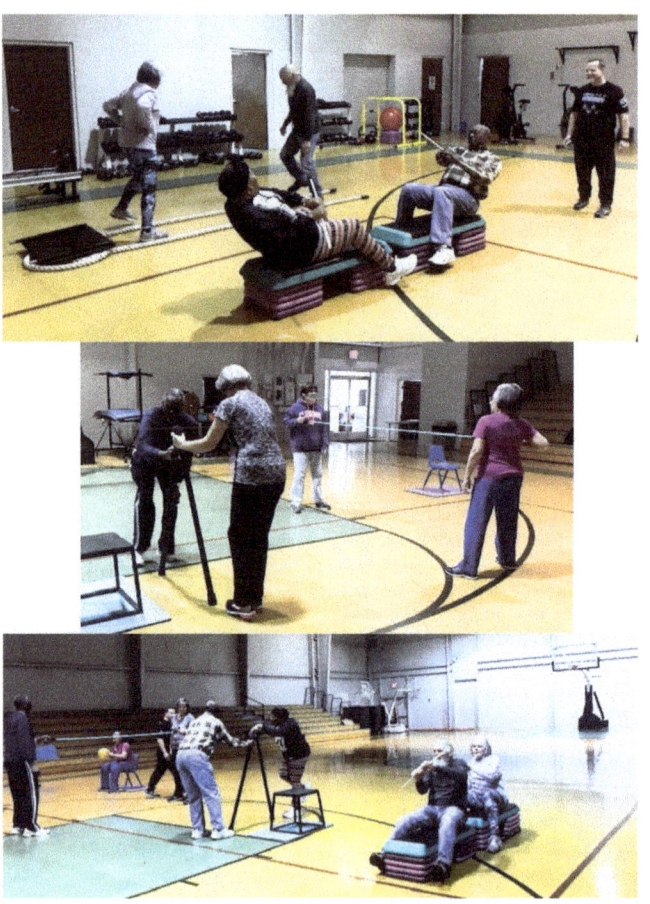

The Overcomers

All dressed out
      With weights in hand –
We stretch, we squat,
      We balance, we stand!

Trained by the best
      We know what to do –
Putting our brains to the test,
      We did all we knew!

Each person remembered
      One piece of the part...
We worked out like pros –
      One mind and one heart ❤️.

We finished in tact,
      And so very relieved,
Then Ruby reminded us –
      We just needed to breathe!

We came and we conquered
      Without trophy 🏆 or cup.
Look at the odds we overcame
      By just getting up!

Butchart Gardens

Dragonflies

Dragonflies dance
    On the breeze in the sun.
Drifting and gliding -
    They move as if one.

They capture my thoughts,
    My heart, and my eyes.
My soul leaps to dance
    With the dragonflies.

Lift with the wind,
    Flap my wings, take to flight!
The moment is now!
    The season just right!

Give me the courage
    To jump at the chance
To leave earth below
    And join in the dance.

Butchart Gardens

If I Could

If I could I'd grant your wish
    Whatever it might be.
I'd give you the desires of your heart
    If it were up to me.

I'd grant your wish to hear you laugh
    And see the smile upon your face.
I'd grant you precious memories
    That time cannot erase.

But some things are not up to me –
    They all depend on you.
So speak your wish and watch to see
    All your dreams come true!

Butchart Gardens

Dreamers

Dreamers dream of what might be.
    They see the things some never see.
They hear the tune of love's sweet song
    And bask in meadows all day long.

With daily woes left far behind,
    They flow through life with peace of mind.
I travel there from time to time,
    And claim the dreamer's life as mine.
A welcome change from cares and woes –
    I close my eyes, and off I go.

And when it's time to come back home
    A little part of me still roams –
Through the meadows, across the streams
    In the Land of Peaceful Dreams.

Dare to dream

    And if you do...

Watch to see

    Your dreams come true.

Nothing Else to Do

There has to be a challenge,
*   An idea, or just a dream.*
A writer needs a plot,
*   Pen and paper, and a theme.*
A painter needs a brush,
*   Canvas, paper, or a wall.*
A hiker needs a trail
*   Winding up a mountain tall.*
A builder needs some space,
*   A blueprint, and lots of tools.*
A chemist needs a lab,
*   Test tubes, theories, crazy rules.*
Like the others, there's the dreamer –
*   Kind of like me and you.*
A dreamer needs his dreams
*   Or he'd have nothing else to do.*

Blow

Blow through this place
    Like never before –
Open the windows,
    Swing wide the doors.

Blow off the dust!
    Clear up the air!
Turn over tables!
    Dislodge the chairs!

Blow over us –
    Your wind in our wings.
Take us higher –
    Above earthly things.

Take us to heights
    Beyond human endeavor,
Where all hearts unite
    In worship forever!

"Old Folks are Fossils" / Glean Wisdom

Glean from the fossils –
 There's wisdom there.
Expertise and compassion –
 So much to share!

The "hows" and the "whys",
 Even "why-nots" –
Like "don't touch the stove
 when the burner's hot".

Sounds very basic,
 But basics we've missed.
We've converted life
 To a "dos" and "don'ts" list.

Let's get back to basics –
Respect and concern.
Hear the heart of the fossil.
There's so much to learn.

Let their mistakes
Be a road to avoid.
Receive what they say
Without being annoyed.

Pearson Falls

Then climb to the top
On the success of the past.
Complete the journey
As a joy – not a task.

Learn how to live,
To love, and to care.
Yes, glean from the fossils –
There's wisdom there.

Written for the generations yet to come.

"Ask your parents what it was like before you were born; ask the old-ones, they'll tell you a thing or two."

Deuteronomy 32:7 (The Message)

Butchart Gardens

Ponder Days

Yonder days have become ponder days:
  When did I get my mother's age?
When did my eyesight start to fade?
  When did my body turn the page?
The years they slip by quickly now –
  What I used to could – I can't.
The little kid inside of me
  Says, "let's go!" but knows it shan't.
So in my dreams I jump and run,
  Catch fireflies, and climb trees.
I can do this from the porch swing
  For as many hours as I please.
On the breeze there is a whisper
  That my failing ears can hear,
"I love that child within you
  As I've watched her year to year."
"It's that child that brings Me pleasure."
  Then I recognize the voice –
It's my Father Who created me
  "You are My child. You are My choice."
How can that be? It's only me.
  But my Father says I'm His.
Amazed with awe and wonder
  He gives me days to ponder this.

Now each day becomes a wonder
  Full of thankfulness and praise,
Reflecting on His goodness,
  Enjoying these ponder days!

What's the Rush?

Linger here a little longer.
     Rest in Me. I'll make you stronger.
Watch the breeze blow through the trees.
     Watch Me dance among the leaves.
Then close your eyes and take My hand,
     And we will dance as lovers can –
Heart-to-Heart and Face-to-Face
     Captured in the sweet embrace.
Hear Me whisper in your ear,
     "You're the treasure I hold most dear."

I want to say, "How can that be?
     Who am I? It's only me."
But the words could not come out,
     You held me close, erased all doubt.
And so, I'll rest in Your embrace.
     For me there is no better place.

Thank you, God, for asking the question,
having this conversation, and the dance.
You are my heart's desire.

A Place Beyond

I know there is a place beyond
Every doubt and fear.
A place where joy can override
Every hurt and tear.

A place where hearts can understand
What words alone can't say.
A place so deep, and love so strong
It can't be explained away.

A place so near and yet so far ...
A pathway with no stairs.
A place beyond our wildest dreams ...
Perhaps I'll meet you there.

The "Other" Place

You've brought us to an "Other" Place,
    Beyond all we can see and feel –
A place where time does not exist,
    Yet it's a place that is so real.

My head says, "This cannot be so
    In a world that's so dark and drear."
My heart says, "Where else would we go?
    Why would we want to leave here?"

So often we'd visit that "Other" Place
    And share what He showed us there.
We'd sit and talk for hours
    About His tender loving care.

Our visits got more intimate
    As we met God day to day.
We longed to be in His presence.
    Oh, how we'd wish we could stay.

So, stay you did in that "Other" Place.
    Your heart's desire was to see His face.
You ran the course, and finished the race.
    One day I'll join you, by His grace.

Dedicated to my husband, Don, who met his Creator face to face on February 13th 2024.

Step Through the Gate

Go beyond me –
    Step through the gate.
Go explore life.
    It's not too late.

Ponder the things
    Worth pond'ring for.
Look for the Truth –
    Go back for more!
Live in the Light –
    There's so much there.
Joy, peace, and love –
    Enough to share!

Share it with friends,
Family, and foe.
Spread it around
Where 'er you go.

Watch as the night
Turns into day,
Darkness to light,
Work into play.

Catawba Falls

Light has a way
To help us see
Paths in the woods,
Forest for trees,

Flowers to smell,
      Birds on the wing,
Life that's so full
      With every good thing.

Step past the gate.
      Go beyond me.
Go and become
      All you can be.

Thank you for taking this walk in the garden.
May you be blessed for joining me on this stroll, and
may it inspire you to venture through the gate
into a garden of your own,
to discover the wonder of life
and all the goodness of God.

Butchart Gardens

About the Author

Susan Stiver is a multifaceted diamond in the rough. From her first wall art with red lipstick, to poetry, sketching, a 40-year career in Neonatal Nursing, motherhood, photography, and mixed media art, this lump of coal now has a superabundance of life treasures to expound upon in literary form. Her passion is to communicate the heart of God through her writing, photography, and art, conveying God's love and desire for each individual to know and be known by Him.

Some say, "In this world, there is no rhyme or reason." But this author has been given rhyme for a reason. It's a creative expression of thoughts, questions, and muses that inspire and encourage others. Her poetry is a dance with words and heart-whispers, scribed on paper with ink. The world is so full of God-wonders. Step into this author's world, and find yourself somewhere in the pages of this book.

Other Books

- He Loves You to Pieces
- A Heart Stirred for Fellowship Co-authored with her husband, Don Stiver

Contact the Author: Susanstiver212@gmail.com

www.ingramcontent.com/pod-product-compliance
Lightning Source LLC
Chambersburg PA
CBHW051522120626
46551CB00012B/1045